THE MYSTERY OF DIVINE SUPPLY

But my God shall supply all your need according to his riches in glory by Christ Jesus.

Philippians 4:19

by

Franklin N. Abazie

The Mystery of Divine Supply
COPYRIGHT 2017 BY Franklin N Abazie
ISBN: 978-1-945-133-47-3

All right reserved. This book or any portion thereof may not be reproduced or used in any manner whatsoever without the express written permission of the publisher, except for the use of brief quotations in a book review. All Bible quotes are from King James Version and others as noted.

Published by: F N ABAZIE PUBLISHING HOUSE- aka, Empowerment Bookstore.

That I may publish with the voice of thanksgiving and tell of all thy wondrous works.
Psalms 26:7

To order additional copies, wholesales
or booking:
Call the Church office (973-372-7518),
or Empowerment Bookstore Hotline (973-393-8518)

Worship address:
343 Sanford Avenue Newark New Jersey 07106
Administrative Head Office address:
33 Schley Street Newark New Jersey 07112
Email:pastorfranknto@yahoo.com
Website www.fnabaziehealingministries.org
Publishing House: www.fnabaziepublishinghouse.org

This book is a production of F N Abazie Publishing House.
A publication Arms of Miracle of God Ministries 2017.
First Edition

CONTENTS

THE MANDATE OF THE COMMISSION iv

ARMS OF THE COMMISSION v

INTRODUCTION vi

CHAPTER 1
1 What Is Divine Supply? 1

CHAPTER 2
2 How To Provoke Divine Supply 10

CHAPTER 3
3 Prayer of Salvation 53

CHAPTER 4
4 About The Author 62

THE MANDATE OF THE COMMISSION

"The moment is due to impact your world through the revival of the healing & miracle ministry of Jesus Christ of Nazareth."

"I am sending you to restore health unto thee and I will heal thee of thy wounds, said the Lord of Host."

ARMS OF THE COMMISSION

1) F N Abazie Ministries-Miracle of God Ministries (Miracle Chapel Intl)

2) F N Abazie TV Ministries: Global Television Ministry Outreach

3) F N Abazie Radio Ministries: Radio Broadcasting Outreach

4) F N Abazie Publishing House: Book Publication

5) F N Abazie Bible School: also called Word of Healing Bible School (W.O.H.B.S)

6) F N Abazie Evangelistic Ass: Miracle of God Ministries: Global Crusade

7) Empowerment Bookstore: Book distribution

8) F N Abazie Helping Hands: Meeting the help of the needy world wide

9) F N Abazie Disaster Recovery Mission: Global Disaster Recovery

10) F N Abazie Prison Ministry: Prison Ministry for all convicts "Second chance"

Some of our ministry arms are waiting the appointed time to commence.

FAVOR CONFESSION

Father thank you for making me righteous and accepted through the blood of Jesus Christ. Because of that, I am blessed and highly favored by God. I am the subject of your affection. Your favor surrounds me as a shield, and the first thing that people see around me is your favored shield. Thank you that I have favor with you and man today. All day long people go out of their way to bless me and help me. I have favor with everyone that I deal with today. Doors that were once closed are now opened for me. I receive preferential treatment, and I have special privileges, I am Gods favored child.

No good thing will he withhold from me. Because of Gods favor my enemies cannot triumph over my life. I have supernatural increase and promotion. I declare restoration to everything that the devil has stolen from my life. I have honor in the midst of my adversaries and an increase in assets, especially in real estate and expansion of territories.

Because I am highly favored by God, I experience great victories, supernatural turnarounds, and miraculous breakthrough in the midst of great impossibilities. I receive recognition, prominence, and honor. Petitions are granted to me even by ungodly authorities. Policies, rules, regulations, and laws are changed and reverse on my behalf.

I win battles that I don't even have to fight, because God fights them for me. This is the day, the set time and the designated moment for me to experience the free favor of God, that profusely and lavishly abound on my behalf in Jesus name. Amen.

INTRODUCTION

"And Jesus took the loaves; and when he had given thanks, he distributed to the disciples, and the disciples to them that were set down; and likewise of the fishes as much as they would."
John 6:12

Although science has always argued about the theory *behind supernatural divine supply*, as a believer, may I submit to you here that besides *divine supply, God is also into miracles, signs, and wonders*. As far as I'm *concerned I do not debate about any doctrine, I only believe in the validity of His Power.*

This publication is written to strengthen and encourage our faith in God. More also to give you confidence and hope in God. Often I tell people to sow a seed of faith *but honestly unless you have a heart of love for God, you never enjoy supernatural divine harvest at the appointed time.*

Divine supply, therefore, is a mystery of the kingdom of God. For *unless we understand how the mysteries of God operates, we will never enjoy supernatural* supply in life.

"Then said the Lord unto Moses, Behold, I will rain bread from heaven for you; and the people shall go out and gather a certain rate every day, that I may prove them, whether they

will walk in my law, or no. And it shall come to pass, that on the sixth day they shall prepare that which they bring in; and it shall be twice as much as they gather daily. **Exodus 16:4-5**

"And Moses said, This shall be, when the Lord shall give you in the evening flesh to eat, and in the morning bread to the full; for that the Lord heareth your murmurings which ye murmur against him: and what are we? your murmurings are not against us, but against the Lord." **Exodus16:8**

For the most part this publication is a book of encouragement to help *our faith and believe system*. Often we go through prevailing circumstances in life *that are quite frightening and challenging. Some folks end up losing hope, others, lose faith, and some others just end up in doubt. But for those of us who dare to believe in the mysteries of signs and wonders,* God will prove Himself *the mighty Name of Jesus Christ.*

We were told....

"But my God shall supply all your need according to his riches in glory by Christ Jesus." **Phil 4:19**

As you read this publication, please neglect my grammar but pay attention to the content of the text as revealed by the Holy Spirit of God. I believe this *small book will provoke the hand of God upon your life. I pray may the mystery of divine supply become your testimony in the Mighty Name of Jesus.*

Have you ever experienced supernatural supply in any form?

It is written, *"I am the Lord: that is my name: and my glory will I not give to another, neither my praise to graven images."* **Isaiah 42:8**

Often some of us are reluctant to share the smallest testimony that happened in their life. As far as I know, every time you refuse to share God's testimony with others that may be your last testimony for a while. *And every time you are excited to share His testimony with others, God performs a mind blowing miracle for you. I pray in the Name of Jesus, that you understand this mystery, and key yourself as a witness in what God will yet do more for you in* life.

HIS DESTINY WAS THE

CROSS....

HIS PURPOSE WAS

LOVE.....

HIS REASON WAS

YOU....

"And Moses said, This shall be, when the Lord shall give you in the evening flesh to eat, and in the morning bread to the full; for that the Lord heareth your murmurings which ye murmur against him: and what are we? your murmurings are not against us, but against the Lord."

Exodus 16:8

DIVINE SUPPLY PRAYER POINTS

*"If ye shall ask any thing in my name,
I will do it.."*
John 14:14

Holy Spirit of God frustrate and disappoint, every one that is against my life and family, in the name of Jesus.

Father Lord destroy every demonic networks and traps against my progress in life in the name of Jesus.

Fire of God, destroy every demonic projection and curses against my life and destiny in the name of Jesus.

Every spell and curses pronounced against my destiny, break, in the name of Jesus.

Hand of God cage every power militating against my rising in life, in the name of Jesus.

Power of God silent every voice raising a counter motion against my elevation, in the mighty name of Jesus.

Blood of Jesus neutralize every spirit of Balaam hired to hinder my life, ministry, and career, the name of Jesus.

Fire of God destroy every curse that I have brought into my life through ignorance and disobedience, break by fire, in the name of Jesus.

Ancient of day destroy every power harassing my ministry in the name of Jesus.

Father God deliver me from invincible forces militating against my life and destiny.

Power of God frustrate every coven and demonic network, designed to frustrate and hinder my success in life, in the name of Jesus.

I dismantle every strong hold designed to imprison my talent in the mighty name of Jesus.

I reject every cycle of frustration, in the name of Jesus.

Power of God paralyze every agent assigned to frustrate my life in the name of Jesus.

Finger of God, grant me supernatural speed against all my contenders in the name of Jesus.

By the blood of Jesus, I destroy every familiar spirit caging my life and career.

Fire of God arrest every demonic agents, assigned to police my destiny and marriage.

By the blood of Jesus, I proclaim no weapon fashioned against me shall ever prosper.

Holy Spirit of God break me through and forward in life in the mighty name of Jesus.

God, smash me and renew my strength, in the name of Jesus.

Holy Spirit, open my eyes to see beyond the visible to the invisible, in the name of Jesus.

Father Lord grant me strength and power in the name of Jesus

O Lord, liberate my spirit to follow the leading of the Holy Spirit.

Holy Spirit, teach me to pray through problems instead of praying about, it in the name of Jesus.

Father Lord, deliver me from the false accusation in life, in the name of Jesus

By the blood of Jesus, every evil spiritual padlock and evil chain hindering my success, be roasted, in the name of Jesus.

By the blood of Jesus I rebuke every spirit of spiritual deafness and blindness in my life, in the name of Jesus.

Father Lord, empower me to dominate the enemy of my destiny in the name of Jesus.

Jesus Christ of Nazareth, heal my infirmities in the name of Jesus

Lord, anoint my eyes and my ears that they may see and hear wondrous things from heaven.

Father Lord, anoint me with power and authority to dominate all my enemies in the name of Jesus.

Fire of God roast every giant rising up against my life and career.

Holy Spirit of God destroy all my oppressors in the name of Jesus.

Angels of good new, bring my good news to me in the mighty name of Jesus.

Every strong man holding me down, lose your hold now in the name of Jesus.

I nullify every demonic prediction over my life in the name of Jesus.

By the blood of Jesus, I flush out every polluted deposit of the enemy in my life.

By the blood of Jesus, I paralyze every enemy of my promotion in the name of Jesus.

Father Lord, destroy any power tormenting my life that is not from you.

Holy Ghost fire, ignite the fire of revival in my life.

By the blood of Jesus, I declare victory over every conflicting trial

By the Blood of Jesus, I command the arrest of every demonic spirit, militating against my life

By the blood of Jesus, I proclaimed the blood of Jesus, over every device of the enemy.

By the blood of Jesus, I revoke stagnation and hardship over my life in the name of Jesus.

Holy Ghost fire, destroy every satanic arrangement in my life, in the name of Jesus.

CHAPTER 1

WHAT IS DIVINE SUPPLY?

Divine Supply *simply means God's timely intervention that defiles all human reasoning and logic. By this I mean, God's supernatural intervention in the affairs of man that defiles all logical, rational, and analytical reasoning in the life of anyone.* This heaven's provision must be unexplainable beyond our human comprehension, otherwise it is not divine supply.

Unless you believe in the reality of divine supply you can never experience it in life. In Mark chapter six, we were told how Jesus Christ couldn't do any miracle because they never believed in the mystery, of *divine supply.* It is written, *"And he could there do no mighty work, save that he laid his hands upon a few sick folk, and healed them. And he marvelled because of their unbelief. And he went round about the villages, teaching."* **Mark 6:5-6**

Anyone that can boldly proclaim *themselves as a believer must also believe in signs and wonders.* For unless you believe in the provision of signs and wonders, you can never partake of the miraculous. *"...ye all are partakers of my grace."* **Phil 1:7**

Divine supply loosely means, *if I may put it this way*, it is the express hand of God in the life and affairs of anyone chosen. *"But my God shall supply all your need according to his riches..."* (Philippians 4:19)

Often most folks do not give God the glory due unto His name. Often God will meet us at our point of need in life yet we tend to deny His doing upon our lives. It is written, "Because they regard not the works of the Lord, nor the operation of his hands, he shall destroy them, and not build them up." **Psalm 28:5**

YOU PROVOKE DIVINE SUPPLY BY BELIEVING IN GOD.

Every time you believe God, you provoke miracles. It is written, *Then said they unto him, What shall we do, that we might work the works of God? Jesus answered and said unto them, This is the work of God, that ye believe on him whom he hath sent.* **John 6:28-29**

We are told in Luke chapter one verse forty five, *"And blessed is she that believed: for there shall be a performance of those things which were told her from the Lord."* (Luke 1:45) When that woman believed God, her cruse of oil never ceased as the Bible records it that all through the time of famine this woman had enough for herself, for her son and for Elijah. (see 1 King 17:9-16)

What is the secret behind divine supply?

~God's prophets

For the most part, *God's prophets, pastors, and apostles* are God's channel to provoke *His divine supply* for us all. It is written, *"Surely the Lord God will do nothing, but he revealeth his secret unto his servants the prophets."* (Amos 3:7) We are told by the book of Hosea, *"And by a prophet the Lord brought Israel out of Egypt, and by a prophet was he preserved."* Hosea 12:13

~Your prayer life

A lifestyle of prayer without ceasing will arrest heaven attention for your timely divine intervention here on earth. Unless you pray without ceasing, you will forever miss your due season. It is written, *"And let us not be weary in well doing: for in due season we shall reap, if we faint not."* **Gal 6:9**

CONDITION TO DIVINE SUPPLY

~BE CONTENT

Unless you are content in life, you will forever miss the blessing of the Lord. We are told "but godliness with contentment is great again." An attitude of contentment is the access key to provoke divine supply in life. Every time you live for other you live forever, but whenever you are selfish in life, you are reduced to self. Unless you are content in life, the blessing of God that makes rich and add no sorrow will never become your portion in life.

~WE MUST GIVE GOD THE GLORY

It is written, "Give unto the Lord the glory due unto his name: bring an offering, and come into his courts." (Psalms 96:8) For unless you engraft the lifestyle of giving God His glory at all times you will forever miss the mystery of the supernatural." It is written "I am the Lord: that is my name: and my glory will I not give to another, neither my praise to graven images." Isaiah 42:8

Often a few of us that are ignorant of this mystery share the glory of God to themselves. That is why God leaves them alone without any tangible testimony or experience of the supernatural in life. If anyone must experience supernatural divine supply in life, then we must give Him the glory due unto His name. We were warned, "Hear ye, and give ear; be not proud: for the Lord hath spoken. Give glory to the Lord your God, before he cause darkness, and before your feet stumble upon the dark mountains, and, while ye look for light, he turn it into the shadow of death, and make it gross darkness." Jeremiah 13:15-16

~CONFESS OF YOUR SIN

Divine supply is the exclusively reserved for the saints of God. If you must experience God, you must confess your sin before Him. The Holy Scripture, teaches that He heareth not sinners. "If we confess our sins, he is faithful and just to forgive us our sins, and to cleanse us from all unrighteousness." 1 John 1:9

~ACKNOWLEDGMENT

Has God done anything at all for you ever since you came to Jesus? We are told, "Nevertheless he left not himself without witness, in that he did good, and gave us rain from heaven, and fruitful seasons, filling our hearts with food and gladness." Acts 14:17

For the most part unless you acknowledge the hand of God for the previous things, God did for you, you will never enjoy the harvest of divine supply. It is written, "Because they regard not the works of the Lord, nor the operation of his hands, he shall destroy them, and not build them up." Psalms 28:5

~BORN AGAIN

As harsh as this may sound to some of us that can't stand it. I repeat you must be born again. That is the order of things in the house of God. If Jesus must turn in your direction, then you must turn to him, first in repentance of your sins. "Return unto me, and I will return unto you, saith the Lord of hosts. But ye said, Wherein shall we return?" (Mal 3:7)

We are told, *"Therefore say thou unto them, Thus saith the Lord of hosts; Turn ye unto me, saith the Lord of hosts, and I will turn unto you, saith the Lord of hosts."* (Zech 1:3) *"Jesus answered and said unto him, Verily, verily, I say unto thee, except a man be born again, he cannot see the kingdom of God."* John 3:3

HINDERANCES TO DIVINE SUPPLY

~Unbelief

As long as you doubt, you will never experience divine supply in life. Even Jesus could not perform miracles because of their unbelief. It is written "And he could there do no mighty work, save that he laid his hands upon a few sick folk, and healed them. And he marveled because of their unbelief. And he went round about the villages, teaching." Mark 6:5-6

~Doubt

One man said to believe in God is a personal choice we make in life. Every time when you operate in doubt, you exempt yourself from experiencing the supernatural in life. If you must provoke the hand of God, then you must believe God for all things in life. It is written, "A double minded man is unstable in all his ways." James 1:8

~Disagreement

Jesus, the miracle worker is a God who operates in agreement. It is written, "Verily I say unto you, whatsoever ye shall bind on earth shall be bound in heaven: and whatsoever ye shall loose on earth shall be loosed in heaven. Again I say unto you, that if two of you shall agree on earth as touching any thing that they shall ask, it shall be done for them of my Father which is in heaven. For where two or three are gathered together in my name, there am I in the midst of them." Matthew 18:18-20

Remember....

"Can two walk together, except they both agreed?" Amos 3:3

~Walking in fear

It is written, "Fear thou not; for I am with thee: be not dismayed; for I am thy God: I will strengthen thee; yea, I will help thee; yea, I will uphold thee with the right hand of my righteousness." Isaiah 41:10

We are commanded to walk in faith and not in fear. For every time you walk in fear you surrender to the devil cheaply. "There is no fear in love; but perfect love casteth out fear: because fear hath torment. He that feareth is not made perfect in love." 1 John 4:18

~Wrong motives

For unless you develop a pure conscience, you will never experience the supernatural in life. It is written, "Holding the mystery of the faith in a pure conscience." (1 Timothy 3:9) For unless you motives are right before God , you will never experience divine supply of God.

CHAPTER 2

HOW DO I PROVOKE DIVINE SUPPLY

"We having the same spirit of faith, according as it is written, I believed, and therefore have I spoken; we also believe, and therefore speak."
2 Corinthians 4:13

I have this favorite sayings, *"before the need arises in our lives, let the supply will be waiting for us."* I boast in faith all the time to make this solid statement. One will think, the above statement is for everybody, no! The above statement is exclusive for *those that daily prevail in prayers, in thanksgiving, and in intercession before the Lord Jesus*. It is written, *"Pray without ceasing."* 1 Theo 5:17

Below is brief methods that anyone can follow to provoke supernatural divine supply.

~ WE MUST DEVELOP A PRAYER LIFE

One will think, just about any new convert can provoke divine supply. Divine supply is a function of devotion, and dedication unto prayer unto God. Anyone without a prayer life, is like a chaff before the wind. It is a prayer life that gives value to our demands. It is written, *"Let my prayer be set forth before thee as incense; and the lifting up of my hands as the evening sacrifice."* **Psalms 141:**.

If you must get enjoy supernatural supply, you must travail in warfare prayer before God. It is written, *"And shall not God avenge his own elect, which cry day and night unto him, though he bear long with them?" I tell you that he will avenge them speedily....* (Luke 18:7-8)

So many years ago, the then Queen of England said: *"I fear nothing but the prayers of John Knox."* Every time you are on fire for God, just about anything answers to your demand. A prayer life in my own opinion is the access key to provoke supernatural divine supply in life.

~ WE MUST DEVELOP AN ATTITUDE OF THANKSGIVING

If you must experience the supply natural supply of God. You must cultivate an attitude of thanksgiving in life. We must develop an attitude to be grateful for the smallest thing to the biggest breakthrough in life. So many people are not thankful for what God has done upon their lives. Every time you are not thankful, frustration and depression takes over your life. *"And when the*

Chapter 2   How Do I Provoke Divine Supply

people complained, it displeased the Lord: and the Lord heard it; and his anger was kindled; and the fire of the Lord burnt among them, and consumed them that were in the uttermost parts of the camp." Number 11:1

For unless *we develop an attitude of thanksgiving,* we make our selves vulnerable to the destroyer. Apostle Paul advised us to *"give no place to the devil"*. It is written, "Neither murmur ye, as some of them also murmured, and were destroyed of the destroyer." 1 Cor 10:10

As long as you are thankful in life you will forever experience divine supply in all sufficiency and at all times. We must learn to *appreciate God for the smallest things in life.*

The beautiful story of the ten leper is a typical example of *an attitude of thanksgiving.* We were told that ten lepers were cleansed but only one had the courage to return to say thank you.

"And Jesus answering said, Were there not ten cleansed? but where are the nine? There are not found that returned to give glory to God, save this stranger. And he said unto him, Arise, go thy way: thy faith hath made thee whole." Luke 17:17-19

Anytime we thank God for any small thing done for us in life, God perfect and completes the miracle for us. It is was the mystery of thanksgiving that Jesus keyed to feed five thousand men excluding women and children.

"And Jesus said, Make the men sit down. Now there was much grass in the place. So the men sat down, in number about five thousand. And Jesus took the loaves; and when he had given thanks, he distributed to the disciples, and the disciples to them that were set down; and likewise of the fishes as much as they would." John 6:10-11

~ WE MUST BELIEVE IN SUPPERNATURAL DIVINE SUPPLY

"You are not permitted to become what you do not believe." I tell *people all the time, you can only experience what you see. God said to Abraham that as far as he can see, God will give it to him.* For the most part unless you *believe in God* you shall not experience divine supply in life. *"Jesus saith unto her, Said I not unto thee, that, if thou wouldest believe, thou shouldest see the glory of God?"* John 11:40

One man said believing is a choice. To *believe in God is a supernatural mystery of the Kingdom that delivers solutions, and answers to any challenge or obstacle in life.* Jesus encouraged the ruler of the synagogue not to doubt but to only believe in God. *"As soon as Jesus heard the word that was spoken, he saith unto the ruler of the synagogue, Be not afraid, only believe."* Mark 5:36

For unless you believe in the mysteries of the kingdom of God, you shall never experience divine supply in life. Jesus said to Thomas. *"Jesus saith unto him, Thomas, because thou hast seen me, thou hast believed: blessed are they that have not seen, and yet have believed."* (John 20:29) No one is permitted to experience *divine supply* in life, especially if they do not believe in supernatural supply in life.

In my own opinion to believe is a choice we make in life. Some people chose to doubt the *"supernatural"* but I chose to *believe in God.* Jesus said it clearly. It is written, *"Jesus said unto him, If thou canst believe, all things are possible to him that believeth. And straightway the father of the child cried out, and said with tears, Lord, I believe; help thou mine unbelief."* Mark 9:23-24

For anyone to provoke the supernatural we must be believe in the birth, ministry, death, and resurrection of our Lord Jesus Christ. We are told, *"For the earnest expectation of the creature waiteth for the manifestation of the sons of God."* Romans 8:19

~ WE MUST BE GRATFUL IN LIFE

Often most people complain and worry about almost everything in their life. As believers we our heart must be at peace. For unless you appreciate God, you will forever suffer frustration in life. *"Because they regard not the works of the Lord, nor the operation of his hands, he shall destroy them, and not build them up."* Psalms 28:5

As far as I know, everything in life starts small. Appreciate God for your small beginning. We are told, *"Though thy beginning was small, yet thy latter end should greatly increase."* (Job 8:7) It is written, *"For who hath despised the day of small things?"* (Zech 4:10) Every time you appreciate God for the smallest thing in life God will exalt you in due time. *"He hath put down the mighty from their seats, and exalted them of low degree."* Luke 1:52

~WE MUST BE HUMBLED IN LIFE AT ALL TIMES

In my own opinion *humility is the key to greatness* in life. If you must become great in life, you must embrace humility as your character in life. It is written, *"But he giveth more grace. Wherefore he saith, God resisteth the proud, but giveth grace unto the humble."* (James 4:6) If you must experience divine supply you must become humbled as a lifestyle. Moses experienced *divine supply* because he was a humbled servant of God. *"Now the man Moses was very meek, above all the men which were upon the face of the earth."* (Number 12:3) The reason you have not experienced divine supply is because you are proud. God resist the proud, but gives more grace to the humbled.

PRAYER POINTS THAT WORK

I cancel my name and that of my family from the death register, with the fire of God, in the name of Jesus.

Every weapon of destruction fashioned against me and my family, be destroyed by the fire of God, in the name of Jesus.

Power of God, fight for me in every area of my life, in Jesus' name.

Every hindrance to my breakthrough, be melted by the fire of God, in the name of Jesus.

Every evil power against me, be scattered by the thunder fire of God, in the name of Jesus.

Father Lord, destroy every evil man/woman in the name of Jesus.

Every failures of the past, be converted to success , in Jesus' name.

Father Lord, let the former rain, the latter rain and Your blessing pour down on me now.

Father Lord, let all the failure turn into success for me, in the name of Jesus.

I receive power from on high and I paralyze all the powers of darkness that are diverting my blessings, in the name of Jesus.

Beginning from this day, I employ the services of the angels of God to open unto me every door of opportunity and breakthroughs, in the name of Jesus.

I will not go around in circles again, I will make progress, in the name of Jesus.

I shall not build for another to inhabit and I shall not plant for another to eat, in the name of Jesus.

I paralyse the powers of the emptier concerning my handiwork, in the name of Jesus.

O Lord, let every locust, caterpillar and palmer-worm assigned to eat the fruit of my labour be roasted by the fire of God.

The enemy shall not spoil my testimony in this programme, in the name of Jesus.

By the blood of Jesus, I reject every backward journey, in the name of Jesus.

By the blood of Jesus, I paralyze every strongman attached to any area of my life, in the name of Jesus.

I pray, Let every agent of shame fashioned to work against my life be paralyzed, in the name of Jesus.

I paralyse the activities of household wickedness over my life, in the name of Jesus.

I quench every strange fire emanating from evil tongues against me, in the name of Jesus.

Father Lord, give me power for maximum achievement.

Heavenly father, give me comforting authority to achieve my goal.

Blood of Jesus Christ, defend and fortify me with Your power.

I paralyse every spirit of disobedience in my life, in Jesus' name.

I refuse to disobey the voice of God, in the name of Jesus.

Every root of rebellion in my life, be uprooted, in Jesus' name.

By the blood of Jesus, I destroy every witchcraft spirit in my life, in the name of Jesus.

Contradicting forces promoting hindrance in my life, die, in Jesus' name.

Every inspiration of witchcraft in my family, be destroyed, in the name of Jesus.

Blood of Jesus, blot out every evil mark of witchcraft in my life, in the name of Jesus.

Every garment put upon me by witchcraft, be torn to pieces, in the name of Jesus.

Angels of God, begin to pursue my household enemies, let their ways be dark and slippery, in the name of Jesus.

Lord, confuse them and turn them against themselves.

By the blood of Jesus, I break every evil unconscious agreement with household enemies concerning my miracles, in the name of Jesus.

Household witchcraft, fall down and die, in the name of Jesus.

Father Lord, drag all the household wickedness to the Dead Sea and bury them there.

Father Lord, I reject to follow the evil pattern of remote control my household enemies.

My life, jump out from the cage of household wickedness, in the name of Jesus.

I command all my blessings and potentials buried by wicked household enemies to be exhumed, in the name of Jesus.

I will see the goodness of the Lord in the land of the living, in the name of Jesus.

Everything done against me to spoil my joy, receive destruction, in the name of Jesus.

Father Lord, as Abraham received favor in Your eyes, let me receive Your favor, so that I can excel in every area of my life.

Lord Jesus, help my shortcoming and infirmities in the name of Jesus.

It does not matter, whether I deserve it or not, I receive immeasurable favor from the Lord, in the name of Jesus.

By the blood of Jesus I receive every blessing God has apportioned to me in the name of Jesus.

My blessing will not be transferred to my neighbor in the name of Jesus.

Father Lord, disgrace every power that is tormenting my breakthrough in the name of Jesus.

Every step I take shall lead to outstanding success, in Jesus' name.

I shall prevail with man and with God in every area of my life, in the name of Jesus.

Every habitation of infirmity in my life, break to pieces, in the name of Jesus.

My body, soul and spirit, reject every evil load, in Jesus' name.

Evil foundation in my life, I pull you down today, in the mighty name of Jesus.

Every inherited sickness in my life, depart from me now, in the name of Jesus.

Every evil water in my body, get out, in the name of Jesus.

By the blood of Jesus, I cancel the effect of every evil dedication in my life, in the name of Jesus.

Holy Ghost fire, immunize my blood against satanic poisoning, in the name of Jesus.

Father Lord, put self control in my mouth, in the name of Jesus.

I refuse to get accustomed to sickness, in the name of Jesus.

Every door open to infirmity in my life, be permanently closed today, in the name of Jesus.

Every power contenting with God in my life, be roasted, in the name of Jesus.

Every power preventing God's glory from manifesting in my life, be paralysed, in the name of Jesus.

I loose myself from the spirit of desolation, in the name of Jesus.

Father Lord break me through in my home, in the name of Jesus.

Father Lord keep in me healthy, in the name of Jesus.

Father Lord break me through in my business, in the name of Jesus.

Let God be God in my economy, in the name of Jesus.

Glory of God, envelope every department of my life, in the name of Jesus.

The Lord that answereth by fire, be my God, in the name of Jesus.

By the blood of Jesus, all my enemies shall scatter to rise no more, in the name of Jesus.

Blood of Jesus, cry against all evil gatherings arranged for my sake, in the name of Jesus.

Father Lord, convert all my past failures to unlimited victories, in the name of Jesus.

Lord Jesus, create room for my advancement in every area of my life.

All evil thoughts against me, Lord turn them to be good for me.

Father Lord, destroy anyone that is against my life in the name of Jesus.

Father Lord, advertise Your dumbfounding prosperity in my life.

Let the showers of dumbfounding prosperity fall in every department of my life, in the name of Jesus.

By the blood of Jesus, I claim all my prosperity in the name of Jesus.

Every door of my prosperity that has been shut, be opened now, in the name of Jesus.

Father Lord, convert my poverty to prosperity, in the name of Jesus.

Father Lord, convert my mistake to perfection, in the name of Jesus.

Father Lord, convert my frustration to fulfillment, in the name of Jesus.

Father Lord, bring honey out of the rock for me, in the name of Jesus.

By the blood of Jesus, I stand against every evil covenant of sudden death, in the name of Jesus.

By the blood of Jesus, I break every conscious and unconscious evil covenant of untimely death, in the name of Jesus.

You spirit of death and hell, you have no document in my life, in the name of Jesus.

You stones of death, depart from my ways, in the name of Jesus.

Father Lord, make me a voice of deliverance and blessing.

By the blood of Jesus, I tread upon the high places of the enemies, in the name of Jesus.

I bind and render useless, every blood sucking demon, in the name of Jesus.

You evil current of death, loose your grip over my life, in the name of Jesus.

By the blood of Jesus, I frustrate the decisions of the evil openers in my family, in the name of Jesus.

Fire of protection, cover my family, in the name of Jesus.

Father Lord, make my way perfect, in the name of Jesus.

Throughout the days of my life, I shall not be put to shame, in the name of Jesus.

By the blood of Jesus, I reject every garment of shame, in the name of Jesus.

By the blood of Jesus, I reject every shoe of shame, in the name of Jesus.

By the blood of Jesus, I reject every head-gear and cap of shame, in the name of Jesus.

Shamefulness shall not be my lot, in the name of Jesus.

Every demonic limitation of my progress as a result of shame, be removed, in the name of Jesus.

Every network of shame around me, be paralysed, in the name of Jesus.

Those who seek for my shame shall die for my sake, in the name of Jesus.

As far as shame is concerned, I shall not record any point for satan, in the name of Jesus.

In the name of Jesus, I shall not eat the bread of sorrow, I shall not eat the bread of shame and I shall not eat the bread of defeat.

No evil will touch me throughout my life, in the name of Jesus.

By the blood of Jesus, In every area of my life, my enemies will not catch me, in the name of Jesus.

By the blood of Jesus, In every area of my life, I shall run and not grow weary, I shall walk and shall not faint.

Father Lord, in every area of my life, let not my life disgrace You.

By the blood of Jesus, I will not be a victim of failure and I shall not bite my finger for any reason, in the name of Jesus.

Holy Spirit of God, Help me O Lord, to meet up with God's standard for my life.

By the blood of Jesus, I refuse to be a candidate to the spirit of amputation, in the name of Jesus.

By the blood of Jesus, with each day of my life, I shall move to higher ground, in the name of Jesus.

Every spirit of shame set in motion against my life, I bind you, in the name of Jesus.

Every spirit competing with my breakthroughs, be chained, in the name of Jesus.

By the blood of Jesus, I bind every spirit of slavery, in the name of Jesus.

By the blood of Jesus, In every day of my life, I disgrace all my stubborn pursuers, in the name of Jesus.

By the blood of Jesus, I bind, every spirit of Herod, in the name of Jesus.

Every spirit challenging my God, be disgraced, in Jesus' name.

Every Red Sea before me, be parted, in the name of Jesus.

By the blood of Jesus, I command every spirit of bad ending to be bound in every area of my life, in the name of Jesus.

By the blood of Jesus, Every spirit of Saul, be disgraced in my life, in the name of Jesus.

By the blood of Jesus, Every spirit of Pharaoh, be disgraced in my life, in Jesus' name.

By the blood of Jesus, I reject every evil invitation to backwardness, in Jesus' name.

By the blood of Jesus, I command every stone of hindrance in my life to be rolled away, in the name of Jesus.

Father Lord, roll away every stone of poverty from my life, in the name Jesus.

Let every stone of infertility in my marriage be rolled away, in the name of Jesus.

Let every stone of non-achievement in my life be rolled away, in the name of Jesus.

My God, roll away every stone of hardship and slavery from my life, in the name of Jesus.

My God, roll away every stone of failure planted in my life, my home and in my business, in the name of Jesus.

You stones of hindrance, planted at the edge of my breakthroughs, be rolled away, in the name of Jesus.

You stones of stagnancy, stationed at the border of my life, be rolled away, in the name of Jesus.

Father Lord, I thank You for all the stones You have rolled away, I forbid their return, in the name of Jesus.

Let the power from above come upon me, in the name of Jesus.

Father Lord, advertise Your power in every area of my life, in the name of Jesus.

Father Lord, make me a power generator, throughout the days of my life, in the name of Jesus.

Let the power to live a holy life throughout the days of my life fall upon me, in the name of Jesus.

Let the power to live a victorious life throughout the days of my life fall upon me, in the name of Jesus.

Let the power to prosper throughout the days of my life fall upon me, in the name of Jesus.

Let the power to be in good health throughout the days of my life fall upon me, in the name of Jesus.

Let the power to disgrace my enemies throughout the days of my life fall upon me, in the name of Jesus.

Let the power of Christ rest upon me now, in the name of Jesus.

Let the power to bind and loose fall upon me now, in the name of Jesus.

Father Lord, let Your key of revival unlock every department of my life for Your revival fire, in the name of Jesus.

Every area of my life that is at the point of death, receive the touch of revival, in the name of Jesus.

Father Lord, send down Your fire and anointing into my life, in the name of Jesus.

Every uncrucified area in my life, receive the touch of fire and be crucified, in the name of Jesus.

Let the fire fall and consume all hindrances to my advancement, in the name of Jesus.

You stubborn problems in my life, receive the Holy Ghost dynamite, in the name of Jesus.

You carry-over miracle from my past, receive the touch of fire in the name of Jesus.

Holy Ghost fire, baptize me with prayer miracle, in Jesus' name.

By the blood of Jesus, Every area of my life that needs deliverance, receive the touch of fire and be delivered, in the name of Jesus.

Let my angels of blessing locate me now, in the name of Jesus.

Every satanic programme of impossibility, I cancel you now, in the name of Jesus.

Every household wickedness and its programme of impossibility, be paralysed, in the name of Jesus.

No curse will land on my head, in the name of Jesus.

Throughout the days of my life, I will not waste money on my health: the Lord shall be my healer, in the name of Jesus.

Throughout the days of my life, I will be in the right place at the right time.

Throughout the days of my life, I will not depart from the fire of God's protection, in the name of Jesus.

Throughout the days of my life, I will not be a candidate for incurable disease, in the name of Jesus.

Every weapon of captivity, be disgraced, in the name of Jesus.

Let every attack planned against the progress of my life be frustrated, in the name of Jesus.

I command the spirits of harassment and torment to leave me, in the name of Jesus.

Lord, begin to speak soundness into my mind and being.

I reverse every witchcraft curse issued against my progress, in the name of Jesus.

I condemn all the spirits condemning me, in the name of Jesus.

Let divine accuracy come into my life and operations, in the name of Jesus.

No evil directive will manifest in my life, in the name of Jesus.

Let the plans and purposes of heaven be fulfilled in my life, in the name of Jesus.

O Lord, bring to me friends that reverence Your name and keep all others away.

Let divine strength come into my life, in the name of Jesus.

Let every stronghold working against my peace be destroyed, in the name of Jesus.

Let the power to destroy every decree of darkness operating in my life fall upon me now, in the name of Jesus.

Lord, deliver my tongue from evil silence.

Lord, let my tongue tell others of Your life.

Lord, loose my tongue and use it for Your glory.

Lord, let my tongue bring straying sheep back to the fold.

Lord, let my tongue strengthen those who are discouraged.

Lord, let my tongue guide the sad and the lonely.

Lord, baptise my tongue with love and fire.

Let every unrepentant and stubborn pursuers be disgraced in my life, in the name of Jesus.

Let every iron-like curse working against my life be broken by the blood of Jesus, in the name of Jesus.

Let every problem designed to disgrace me receive open shame, in the name of Jesus.

Let every problem anchor in my life be uprooted, in Jesus' name.

Multiple evil covenants, be broken by the blood of Jesus, in the name of Jesus.

Multiple curses, be broken by the blood of Jesus, in Jesus' name.

Everything done against me with evil padlocks, be nullified by the blood of Jesus, in the name of Jesus.

Everything done against me at any cross-roads, be nullified by the blood of Jesus, in the name of Jesus.

Let every stubborn and prayer resisting demon receive stones of fire and thunder, in the name of Jesus.

Every stubborn and prayer resisting sickness, loose your evil hold upon my life, in the name of Jesus.

Every problem associated with the dead, be smashed by the blood of Jesus, in the name of Jesus.

I recover my stolen property seven fold, in the name of Jesus.

Let every evil memory about me be erased by the blood of Jesus, in the name of Jesus.

By the blood of Jesus, I disallow my breakthroughs from being caged, in Jesus' name.

Let the sun of my prosperity arise and scatter every cloud of poverty, in the name of Jesus.

I decree unstoppable advancement upon my life, in Jesus' name.

I soak every day of my life in the blood of Jesus and in signs and wonders, in the name of Jesus.

I break every stronghold of oppression in my life, in Jesus' name.

Let every satanic joy about my life be terminated, in the name of Jesus.

I paralyze every household wickedness, in the name of Jesus.

Let every satanic spreading river dry up by the blood of Jesus, in the name of Jesus.

I bind every ancestral spirit and command them to loose their hold over my life, in the name of Jesus.

CONCLUSION

"And Jesus took the loaves; and when he had given thanks, he distributed to the disciples, and the disciples to them that were set down; and likewise of the fishes as much as they would. When they were filled, he said unto his disciples, Gather up the fragments that remain, that nothing be lost." **John 6:11-12**

For the most part, *God is a God of divine supply*. If anyone tells you otherwise do not believe them. *God is a God of signs and wonders, miracles and healing.* We like you to take time out of your busy schedule and become a born again Christian. Especially if you are not a born again believer.

Eccl 12:13-14

Let us hear the conclusion of the whole matter: Fear God, and keep his commandments: for this is the whole duty of man.

For God shall bring every work into judgment, with every secret thing, whether it be good, or whether it be evil.

The entire book will remain a story to everyone who is not ready to make a decision for Jesus Christ. One man said if you failed to plan we have planned to fail in life. We want you to make plans to make heaven.

The bible says in Eccl: 12:14, For God shall bring every work into judgment, with every secret thing, whether it be good, or whether it be evil. If you are a born again Christian; we like to encourage you in your Christian life. If you are not a born again Christian we can help you here receive genuine salvation.

"Therefore if any man be in Christ, he is a new creature: old things are passed away; behold, all things are become new."
2 Cor 5:17

Now repeat this Prayer after me

Say Lord Jesus, I accept you today, as my Lord and my savior, forgive me of my sins wash me with your blood. Right now, I believe, I am sanctified, I am save, I am free, I am free from the Power of sin to serve the Lord Jesus. Thank you Lord for saving me. Amen.

Congratulations: You are now...

A BORN AGAIN CHRISTIAN.

Again I say to you—

CONGRATULATIONS!

What must I do to determine my divine visitation?

To determine divine visitation you must be born again! The word says as many as received him, to them gave He power to become the sons of God. Even to them that believe on his name.

To qualify for divine visitation, do the following with sincerity—

1) Acknowledge that you are a sinner and that He died for you. (Romans 3:23)

2) Repent of your sins. (Acts 3:19, Luke 13:5, 2 Peter 3:9)

3) Believe in your heart that Jesus died for your sin. (Romans 10:10)

4) Confess Jesus as the Lord over your life. (Romans 10:10, Acts 2:21)

Now repeat this Prayer after me

Say Lord Jesus, I accept you today, as my Lord and my savior, forgive me of my sins wash me with your blood. Right now, I believe, I am sanctified, I am save, I am free, I am free from the Power of sin to serve the Lord Jesus. Thank you Lord for saving me. Amen.

Congratulations: You are now...

A BORN AGAIN CHRISTIAN.
Again I say to you—

CONGRATULATIONS!

I adjure you to watch the Spirit of God bear witness with your Spirit confirming His word with signs following. The word says The Spirit itself beareth witness with our spirit, that we are the children of God. Join a bible believing church or join us on our weekly and Sunday worship services at 343 Sanford Avenue, Newark, New Jersey, 07106.

WISDOM KEYS

— Every Productive Society is a society heading to the top.

— Millions of Nigerians run away from Nigeria, very few Nigerians stay in Nigeria.

— My decision to return Nigeria is the will of God for my life.

— My short coming in America after 18 years, trained me to be wise, to think, reflect and reason appropriately.

— If you train your mind to reason it will train your hands to earn money.

— It is absurd to use the money of the heathen to build the kingdom of the living God.

— Every Ministry reveals its agenda and goal either at the beginning or at the end. Be careful of your life it is your first Ministry.

— The average American mind is conditioned for a continual quest to get new things and (discard the former) and throw away old things.

— When I considered well, my BMW jeep became my initial deposit for the work of the ministry in Nigeria.

— Money will never fall from any tree.

— Everyone is waiting for you to change your mind until you change your thinking nothing changes around you.

— Multiple academic degrees in other discipline gave me the chance to think, reflect and reason.

— What so everyone are thinking and reflecting at the moment reveals you to the time and the now factor .

—All events and intents are the product of precise thought processes, accurate reason every event is designed for a designated timeline.

— Wisdom is your ability to think, to create and invent. If you can think wise enough you will come out of penury.

— The distance between you and success is your creative ability to think reason and reflect accurate.

— Success is the result of hard work, commitment resolve and determination learning from past mistakes and failing.

— If you organize your mind you have organized your life and destiny.

— There is a thin line between success and failure. If you look above and beyond you are on your way to success.

— Wealth is your ability to think, power is your ability to reason and success is your ability to be informed.

— If you can make use of your mind by thinking and reasoning God will make use of your life and destiny.

— Think and Be Great.

— Reflect, Reason, Think and Be Great.

— Famous people are born of woman.

— That you will make it is your intention; that you will survive is your resolve, that you will succeed with changes is your determination, personal efforts and hard work.

— No man was born a failure. Lack of vision is the end product of failure.

— Working with mental patients encourages and aspire me to be a productive observant and dedicated to my assignment.

— Successful people are not magicians, it is the will power combined with hard work, and determination and a resolve to succeed that make them succeed.

— In the unequivocal state of the mind, intention is not a location or a position it is the state of the mind.

— So many people think, that they think. The mind is used to think, reflect, and reason. You will remain blind with your eye open until you can see with your mind by thinking.

— There is no favoritism in accurate and precise calculation.

— Although knowledge is power, information is the key and gateway to a great future.

— It will take the hand of God to move the hand of man.

— With the backing of the great wise God, nothing will disconnect you from your inheritance.

— As long as you have wisdom and understanding of God, Satan and evil cannot manipulate your life and destiny.

— You have come this far by yourself judgment and decision you have made in the past, now lean and listen to God for another dimension of greatness.

— Great people are common people it is extra ordinary effort and the price of sacrifice that produces greatness.

— As a mental direct care worker I saw a great pastor and a motivational speaker within myself.

— Menial job does not reduce your self-worth, until you resolve to achieve greatness see greatness in all you do; you will never count in your community.

— The principle of Jesus will solve your gambling and addiction problems.

— The man of Jesus will lead you into heaven.

— Everyone have their self-appraisal and what they think about you. Until you discover yourself other opinion about you will alter the real you.

— Supervisors and directors are just a position in the chain of command in a work place. Never allow your supervisor hierarchy to alter your opinion about yourself.

— Everyone can come out of debt if they make up their mind.

— That I am not a decision maker at work does not diminish my contribution to my world.

— Although it appears like it was a poor decision to accept a direct care employment at a psychiatric hospital as I reflect of my nine years of experience, it became apparent that I have learnt and experienced enough for my next assignment in life.

— Self-encouragement and determination is a resolve of the heart.

— If you are determined to make a difference, and do the things that make a difference you will eventually make a difference.

— Good things do not come easy.

— Short cuts will cut your life short.

— Those who look ahead move ahead.

— Life is all about making an impact. In your life time strive to make an impact in your community.

— Make friends and connect with people who are moving ahead of you in life.

— If you can look around well you have come a long way in your life, made a lot of difference and realized a lot of success in life.

— If you are my old friend, hurry up to reach out to me before I become a stranger to you.

— Everything I am blessed with inspirations from God, that change my definition and interpretation of the world around me.

— I thought I was stagnant and lonely until I looked around and noticed my children running around and my wife cooking.

— At 40 I resigned my Job to seek the Lord forever.

— My ministry took a drastic rise to the top when the wisdom of God visited me with knowledge and understanding.

— You will be a better person, if you understand the characteristics of your personality – your mood swings, attitudes, and habits.

— It is the seed of love you sow into the heart of a child and a woman that you reap in due time.

— Love is not selfish, love share everything including the concealed secrets of the mind.

— As long as you have a prayer life and a bible; you will never feel lonely, rejected, and idle in the race of life.

— When good friends disconnect from you, let them go, they might have seen something new in a different direction.

— Confidence in yourself and in God is the only way to bring you out of captivity.

— Never train a child to waste his/her time.

— The mind is the greatest assets of a great future.

— You walk by common sense run by principles and fly by instruction.

— Those who fly in flight of life fly alone.

— Up in the air you are alone. No one can toll you accept the compass of knowledge and information.

— I have seen a towing vehicle I have seen a towing ship I have never seen a tolling airplane.

— I exercise my judgment and make a decision every minute of the day.

— Decisions are crucial, critical and vital with reference to your future.

— So many people wish for a great future. You can only work towards a great future.

— Your celebrity status began when you discovered your talent. What are you good at? Work at it with all commitment.

— Prayers will sustain you but the wisdom of God will prosper you.

— When I met Oyedepo, his teachings changed my perspective. But when I met Ibiyeomie; His teaching changed my perception.

— I will be successful in ministry if only I concentrate and focus my energy in the work of the ministry.

— It took the late Dr. Vincent Pearle Norman's book to open my mind towards kingdom success.

CHAPTER 3

PRAYER OF SALVATION

"Neither is there salvation in any other: for there is none other name under heaven given among men, whereby we must be saved."
Acts 4:12

What must I do to determine my divine visitation?

To be saved we must be born again! The word says as many as received him, to them gave He power to become the sons of God. Even to them that believe on his name.

To qualify for divine visitation, do the following with sincerity—

1) Acknowledge that you are a sinner and that He died for you. (Romans 3:23)

2) Repent of your sins. (Acts 3:19, Luke 13:5, 2 Peter 3:9)

Chapter 3   Prayer of Salvation

3) Believe in your heart that Jesus died for your sin. (Romans 10:10)

4) Confess Jesus as the Lord over your life. (Romans 10:10, Acts 2:21)

Now repeat this Prayer after me

Say Lord Jesus, I accept you today, as my Lord and my savior, forgive me of my sins wash me with your blood. Right now, I believe, I am sanctified, I am save, I am free, I am free from the Power of sin to serve the Lord Jesus. Thank you Lord for saving me. Amen.

Congratulations: You are now...

A BORN AGAIN CHRISTIAN.
Again I say to you—

CONGRATULATIONS!

I adjure you to watch the Spirit of God bear witness with your Spirit confirming His word with signs following. The word says The Spirit itself beareth witness with our spirit, that we are the children of God.

MIRACLE CARE OUTREACH

*"...But that the members should have
the same care one for another"*
1 Corinthians 12:25

We are all members of the body of Christ. Jesus commanded us to love our neighbor as ourselves. This includes caring for one another as a member of one body. True love is expressed in caring and giving. The word says for God so Love He gave….

Reach out to someone in need of Jesus, help someone in crisis find Christ. Look out and prove your love to Jesus by caring and inviting your friends and associates to find Jesus the Healer.

Invite your friends to our Home Care Cell Fellowship (Miracle chapel Intl Satellite fellowship) In the USA at 33 Schley Street, Newark, New Jersey, 07112. Home Care Cell fellowship Group meets every Tuesday at 6:00pm-7:00pm.

If you are in Nigeria—**MIRACLE OF GOD MINISTRIES**, aka "**MIRACLE CHAPEL INTL**" Mpama –Egbu-Owerri Imo state Nigeria.

LIFE IS NOT ALL ABOUT DURATION— BUT ITS ALL ABOUT DONATION

What does the above statement mean?....

Life consists not in the accumulation of material wealth. (Luke 12:15) But it's all about liberality...meaning - what you can give and share with others. Proverb11:25. When you live for others—You live forever - because you out live your generation by the legacy you live behind after you depart into glory to be with the Lord. But when you live to yourself - you are reduced to self—you are easily forgotten when you die and depart in glory. Permit me to admonish you today to live your life to be a blessing to a soul connected to you today. I want you to know that so many souls are connected and looking up to you, and through you so many souls will be saved and rescued from destruction. Will you disciple someone today to find Jesus Christ?

As a genuine Christian; it is your duty to evangelize Jesus Christ to all you meet on your way. Jesus is still in the healing business-Jesus is still doing miracles from time of old to now. Therefore tell someone about Jesus Christ today, disciple and bring them to Church. (John 1:45) Philip findeth Nathanael....

Please to prove the sincerity of your love for God today; please become a soul winner. The dignity of your Christianity is hidden in your boldness to proclaim and evangelize Jesus Christ to all you meet on your way. There is a question mark on the integrity of your Christianity until you become a life soul winner. Invite someone to join us worship the Lord Jesus this coming Sunday. Amen.

MIRACLE OF GOD MINISTRIES

PILLARS OF THE COMMISSION

We Believe Preach and Practice the following:

1) We believe and preach Salvation to every living human being

2) We believe and preach Repentance and forgiveness of sins

3) We believe and preach the baptism of the Holy Spirit and Spiritual gifts

4) We believe and teach the Prosperity

5) We believe and preach Divine Healing and Miracles (Signs &Wonder)

6) We believe and preach Faith

7) We believe and proclaim the Power of God (Supernatural)

8) We believe and proclaim Praise& Worship to God

9) We believe and preach Wisdom

10) We believe and preach Holiness (Consecration)

11) We believe and preach Vision

12) We believe and teach the Word of God

13) We believe and teach Success

14) We believe and practice Prayer

15) We believe and teach Deliverance

These 15 stones form the Pillars of Our Commission. Become part of this church family and follow this great move of God.

MY HEART FELT PRAYER FOR YOU

It is my prayer that you testify today about the goodness of the Lord. I desire for you to have an encounter with our Lord Jesus Christ. More especially , I desire for you to experience divine supply of God in a breakthrough fashion upon your personal life.

Now let me pray for you:

Heavenly father may today be a day of new beginning for this precious love one. Lord God of heaven open a new chapter in the life of this precious love one reading this book today. May all their prayers be answered in the mighty name of Jesus. We thank you Jesus for hearing us. In Jesus mighty name. Amen.

WHAT TO DO WHEN MIRACLE SEEMS TO BE DELAYED:

1) Praise God even in times of trouble, trial, and tribulations.

2) Be expectant- expect God to move beyond imagination.

3) Be willing and Obedient-God look at your obedient in times of delay.

4) Be focus—God expect us to pay relevant attention to details.

5) Do not quit- If we must emerge winners, quitting is not an option.

6) Be positive—it can only get better so be positive.

7) Be optimistic--- Your case is different so be optimistic in life.

8) Develop all possibility mentality—Every limitation is within you faith.

UNDERSTANDING YOUR DUE SEASON

There is always a season for everyone. Often we miss our season, either because we are not paying attention, or because we are ignorant of the truth. *I advise you to always make it a habit to rejoice with others every time someone gets a testimony go out your way to share their testimony with them.* God does not look like the way man look. God looks into the heart. Every time you are truly thankful and grateful for some one's testimony, you are next in line for a miracle.

CHAPTER 4
ABOUT THE AUTHOR

Rev Franklin N Abazie is the founding and Presiding Pastor of Miracle of God Ministries with headquarters in Newark, New Jersey USA and a branch church in Owerri- Imo State Nigeria. He is following the footsteps of one of his mentors, Oral Roberts (Healing Evangelist) of the blessed memory. The Lord passed Oral Roberts healing mantle two days before he went to be with the Lord at age 91 into the hand of healing evangelist-Rev Franklin N Abazie in a vision.

In all his services the Power and Presence of God is present to heal all in his audience. He is an ordained man of God with a Healing Ministry reviving the healing and miracle ministry of Jesus Christ of Nazareth.

Pastor Franklin N Abazie, is called by God with a unique mandate: **"THE MOMENT IS DUE TO IMPACT YOUR WORLD THROUGH THE REVIVAL OF THE HEALING & MIRACLE MINISTRY OF JESUS CHRIST OF NAZARETH**

"I AM SENDING YOU TO RESTORE HEALTH UNTO THEE AND I WILL HEAL

THEE OF THY WOUNDS. SAID THE LORD OF HOST"

Rev. Abazie is a gifted ardent Teacher of the word of God who operates also in the office of a Prophet, generating and attracting undeniable signs & wonders, special miracles and healings, with apostolic fireworks of the Holy Ghost. He is the founding and presiding senior Pastor of this fast growing Healing ministry. He has written over 86 inspirational, healing and transforming books covering almost all aspect of divine healing and life. He is happily married and blessed with children.

BOOKS BY REV FRANKLIN N ABAZIE

1) The Outcome of Faith
2) Understanding the secret of prevailing Prayers
3) Commanding Abundance
4) Understanding the secret of the man God uses
5) Activating my due Season
6) Overcoming Divine Verdicts
7) The Outcome of Divine Wisdom
8) Understanding God's Restoration Mandate
9) Walking in the Victory and Authority of the truth
10) Gods Covenant Exemption
11) Destiny Restoration Pillars
12) Provoking Acceptable Praise
13) Understanding Divine Judgment
14) Activating Angelic Re-enforcement
15) Provoking Un-Merited Favor
16) The Benefits of the Speaking faith
17) Understanding Divine Arrangement
18) Put your faith to work
19) Developing a positive attitude in life
20) The Power of Prevailing faith
21) Inexplicable faith
22) The intellectual components of Redemption.
23) Dominating Controlling Spirit
24) Understanding Divine Prosperity
25) Understanding the secret of the man God Uses
26) Retaining Your Inheritance
27) Never give up hope
28) Commanding Angelic Escorts
29) The winner's faith
30) Understanding Your Guardian Angels
31) Overcoming the Dominion of Sin
32) Understanding the Voice of God

33) The Outstanding benefits of the Anointing
34) The Audacity of the Blood of Jesus
35) Walking in the Reality of the Anointing
36) The Mystery of Divine supply
37) Understanding Your Harvest Season
38) Activating Your Success Buttons
39) Overcoming the forces of Darkness
40) Overcoming the devices of the devil
41) Overcoming Demonic agents
42) Overcoming the sorrows of failure
43) Rejecting the Sorrows of failure
44) Resisting the Sorrows of Poverty
45) The Restoring broken Marriages.
46) Redeeming Your Days
47) The force of Vision
48) Overcoming the forces of ignorance
49) Understanding the sacrifice of small beginning
50) The might of small beginning
51) Praying in the Spirit
52) Dominating controlling Spirits
53) Breaking the shackles of the curse of the law
54) Covenant keys to answered prayers
55) Wisdom for Signs & Wonders
56) Wisdom for generational Impact
57) Wisdom for Marriage Stability
58) Understanding the number of your Days
59) Enforcing Your Kingdom Rights
60) Escaping the traps of immoralities
61) Escaping the trap of Poverty
62) Accessing Biblical Prosperity
63) Accessing True Riches in Christ
64) Silencing the Voice of the Accuser
65) Overcoming the forces of oppositions
66) Quenching the voice of the avenger
67) Silencing demonic Prediction & Projection
68) Silencing Your Mocker

69) Understanding the Power of the Holy Ghost
70) Understanding the baptism of Power
71) The Mystery of the Blood of Jesus
72) Understanding the Mystery of Sanctification
73) Understanding the Power of Holiness
74) Praying in the spirit
75) Activating the Forces of Vengeance
76) Appreciating the Mystery of Restoration
77) Covenant Keys to Answered Prayers
78) Engaging the mystery of the blood
79) Commanding the Power of the Speaking faith
80) Uprooting the forces against Your Rising
81) Overcoming mere success syndrome
82) Understanding Divine Sentence
83) Understanding the Mystery of Praise
84) Understanding the Author of Faith
85) The Mystery of the finisher of faith
86) Where is your trust?

MIRACLE OF GOD MINISTRIES

*NIGERIA CRUSADE
2012*

MIRACLE OF GOD MINISTRIES

NIGERIA CRUSADE 2012

MIRACLE OF GOD MINISTRIES

*NIGERIA CRUSADE
2012*

www.ingramcontent.com/pod-product-compliance
Lightning Source LLC
Chambersburg PA
CBHW021157080526
44588CB00008B/381